THE EXCELLENT ASSEMBLY

Other Works by Robert McDowell

Poetry

Sweet Wolf: Selected & New Poems
The World Next to This One
On Foot, In Flames.
The Pact (limited edition)
The Diviners
Quiet Money
At the House of the Tin Man (Chapbook)
History, Hardware and Romance, with prints by Michael Aakhus (limited, edition)

Fiction

Emily & Virginia
His Singing Cowboy Days
How I Came To Know Fish, by Ota Pavel, stories translated with Jindriska Badal

Criticism

Poetry as Spiritual Practice: Reading, Writing and Using Poetry in Your Daily Rituals, Aspirations and Intentions
The Reaper Essays, with Mark Jarman
Sound and Form in Modern Poetry, with Harvey Gross

Nonfiction

The More We Get Together: The Sexual and Spiritual Language of Love

Editor

One Man Boat: The Writing of George Hitchcock, with Joseph Bednarik and Mark Jarman
Cowboy Poetry Matters: From Abilene to the Mainstream: Contemporary Cowboy Writing
Poetry After Modernism

e-Books

Before I Pray (a Kevin Killgallen mystery)
Haiku: How To Write It in Minutes (writer's guide)
Change Writer's Block to Writer's Stock You Can Take to the Bank: 10 Steps to Curing Writer's Block Forever (writer's guide)
Sonnets: How To Write Them in Minutes (writer's guide)

THE EXCELLENT ASSEMBLY

Poems Commemorating
the 25th Anniversary of 9/11

ROBERT McDOWELL

HLP

Homestead Lighthouse Press
Akron, Ohio & Ashland, Oregon

Names: Robert McDowell, author.

Library of Congress Control Number: 2026937214

ISBN 978-1-950475-49-0

Homestead Lighthouse Press
796 W. Market Street, Apt. C
Akron, Ohio 44303
www.homesteadlighthousepress.com

Distributed by Homestead Lighthouse Press, HLP Distribution, Amazon.com, Barnes & Noble

Cover & Book Design: Ray Rhamey, Ashland, OR

Homestead Lighthouse Press gratefully acknowledges the generous support of its readers and patrons.

Contents

The Excellent Assembly, as described in the Purana, signifies a remarkable gathering of wise and virtuous individuals united for discussion or a common goal. It is metaphorically illuminated by the sun, symbolizing enlightenment.

Foreword

Mick J. Earpp, Poet, Archaeologist, Influencer

No book of poetry in 2026 or any year will be more timely and important than *The Excellent Assembly.*

A quarter-century in the making, this stunning collection of closely woven lyrical narratives honors those who lost their lives and those whose actions endure and inspire us as we look back at the 9/11 catastrophe, which changed not only our American lives, but lives everywhere. These poems bear witness to the unforgettable songs inside these stories.

ON THE GROUND

Glendale, CA.

For the last time, get in the car!
Your sister will be standing there
Wondering where we are. Maria!
Stop with the crying! What's wrong?

What if she doesn't come?

Don't be silly. I talked to her
On the plane. She's coming.

What if she doesn't land?
Honey, she's going to land just fine.

She wasn't on that plane.

There could be more!

Don't be silly. Hurry up!
Get in the car.

Cabinet Member in Love

My heart was never better. The planes go down
And it's a tragic opportunity.
I mean, too bad so many lives go out,

But praise the Lord, we're blessed with many more!
Fate. It's got to be--profit in
A place we couldn't touch before.

When I was a kid I used to pass a store
That had the greatest toys! I got my share
On all the special days, but wanted more.

Sometimes I'd watch another boy come out
Of there with something—anything—and oh
I hated him! I wanted what he had.

I'd follow him and jump him if I knew
That I could take him. Then his toy was mine.
There's nothing like it, getting what you want!

Timid victims never said a word,
Accepting their fate, while others spilled their guts.
A phone call to my parents brought me up

On charges, but I learned a lesson I
Have always trusted: Lie. You know, it works!
It doesn't matter if a camera

Has caught you dead to rights. Just tell your lie,
And tell it till they tire of asking you.
That's all you need to do! And who's to say

A lie can't be the truth? I'd better call
The president and get him to a place
Where he can ride this out. The less he says,

You know, the better. Time to pad my bank
Account with contracts for the company
I "used" to run. I bet my dad would smile

To see me now. "A country," he would say.
"That's better than a toy store, son!" I get
a little misty thinking of my dad

cheerleading me on like that. So much to do!
I wonder what we'd gain by shooting down
Some planes before we ground them. Fear is a friend

Of government. We're going to do the things
We've dreamed about. Oh, smell that morning air!
Smells like sweet exhaust, five bucks a gallon.

FLIGHT ONE

PILOT TO CO-PILOT

When your day begins
With a sighting
Of a turkey vulture–
Not on the highway
Devouring road kill,
But all alone
In a suburb,
Deliberately strolling
Up the sidewalk–
Maybe you should
Take it as an omen.

I saw such a thing
This morning, just three
Blocks from my house.
I was driving
My daughter to school.
"Look, Daddy!," she said.
We slowed the car
To a crawl, keeping pace
With the unhurried bird.
"I thought they lived
Far away in the woods,"
She said. "Why
Is it here?"

"Beats me," I said.
"Look at it! That
Is one ugly, sinister critter.

You're right, honey.
Its home should be
The Unknown,
Away from people,
People like us."

ENTERTAINER

If I were home again, if I were home,
I'd entertain no more in foreign states.
The troops would have to make it without my help.
My writers are my family, and they
Are going with me. This is a consequence
That none of them expected. Poor Eugene,
Who joined us just a month ago. He knows
He'll never see Chicago or his wife
Again. I guess this has to be my fault
Because I run the show. I tell them when
And how to live. America listens to me.
I wonder how hung-over everyone
Will be when I'm no longer on TV,
When I'm no longer making of myself
A bridge between anxiety and sleep.
I wish by telling jokes we'd turn this plane around,
But nothing sounds too funny in my head.
I'll go on talking to myself like this
Until the end. If I were home, if I....

Domme

I know the type. I've racked a few.
They're special cases, having lived abroad
For many years. They grow to like the States
Because what's not to like? They're well financed,
And everybody knows what money does;
It makes imagination possible.
To them I am the perfect long-legged dream
Of Yankee decadence. They kneel before
Me eager to endure whatever I
Decide to do to them. They're guilty in
Their hunger. "Purge me!" one kept yelling as
I warmed his chest with piss. Another liked
To watch me whip his friend, who otherwise
Was dominant in their relationship.
A third would see me every year or so
For Bengal Marathon, my special that
Is only for initiates who have
Experience—and pockets deep enough
To pay the two grand I require.
This life is good, a life of dishing out
And hauling in. So many men are fools,
Destructive in their jealousies and greed.
When women rule relationships, they work.

Too Late To Tell

I never said enough,
I seldom made him feel
That mostly it was love
That made our pact, our deal.

Mostly it's been words
We spin and hide behind;
One warbles, one's a dirge.
We seek but never find.

We switch, we play each other,
We keep our distance, so.
In solitude is power—
We let that feeling grow.

We're miserable at bonding,
We've got our comfort zones,
Like mommy and like daddy
We'll fumble until we're bones.

We'll grumble that we're ready
For something more than this,
But that's just acting giddy.
It's a lie, it's hit and miss.

Some loves might last forever,
Some only for a day.
Some build, and some will never
Cross over, settle, stay.

Little Girl

Awesome noise!
Mom pats my knee
And smiles the way
She does when she
Is telling me
It's all ok.
We're moving
Faster, faster than
I've ever been
On my bicycle.
A man
Across the aisle
Smiles at me.
He's handsome. Dark.
I smile back.

Now
We're climbing,
Fast as a rocket ship!
My baby brother
Cries. Mom says his ears
Are hurting. *Open*
And close your mouth,
She says, and demonstrates.
Like this.
The handsome man
Gives me a stick
Of gum. He smiles.
He points at the gum,

Then his ears. His
Teeth are so white!
Maybe

He's a dentist.
Chewing gum
Makes the pain
In our ears
Go away.

My brother stops
With his crying.
I watch his eyes
Get fluttery and close,
His head on mom's shoulder.

I open
My airport book
To color the planes,
The crew and passengers.
I know!
I'll make one passenger
The man who gave
Me gum.
I look at him,
Smiling,
But he is in
The aisle.
He's saying something

To a flight attendant.
They're in
The cockpit now.
How nice!
He wants to see
How the plane flies
And they're showing him.

Maybe later mom
Can ask if they
Will show me, too.
Oh, wouldn't that
Be something to tell
Daddy when he meets us!
Be patient,
Mom would say
If she weren't asleep.

Irritating Seat Mate

A man who says he loves an early flight
Will also tell you how his mother-in-law
Can move right in for all he cares.
Removing his ear phones, acknowledging
That genius-circuit flashing in his head,
He has to share the very latest thing
That just occurred to him.

I wonder if the smile he's wearing hurts.
When I was younger I'd be steaming now,
Stuck in the back of a plane beside a poster guy
For Rotary who won't shut up.
I tell you I could set my watch by him.

"I told my wife on the phone last night, honey,
I said, it's time we took a trip. Think Jamaica."

He asks me if I've ever been.

No, I say, but I know someone who has.
She couldn't stand the poverty.
I thought this might provide a dampening effect,
Might cast a gritty shadow between
His irritating cheerfulness and me,
But I am disappointed.
"Yup, I told her,
Start packing for Jamaica, babe.
(And then, conspiratorially, leaning in,)
I have to give her something, make a fuss,

Because last night—it's the darnedest thing—
I lost my wedding ring. It hasn't been
Off my finger in years and years,
But there I was in that motel bed,
Slowly stroking myself as I like to do
When I wake up. Whoa!
It didn't feel the same. My finger was bare.
I put a search into that room
A custom agent would have approved of.
I called the desk.
                                        If it's here
We'll find it, they said.

"So there was nothing more to do
But check out and make this flight.
I'm glad I did, especially after
Meeting up with a guy like you.
You're good company! I bet
You hear that all the time.
I wish that flight attendant would get here
With that cart, though. My stomach's growling."

To take his mind off of his stomach,
And yes, to mess with him,
I try to tell him about the
Born Once/Born Twice theory of William James.
I don't care that he's never heard of William James,
Explaining that people born once just scratch life's surface,
That they're naïve, innocent as children, even silly,
While people born twice lean toward the cynical,
The darkness, the murky currents we all swim in.
Surely he grasps the significance,
But as I search his eyes for a sign
I see that nothing I say phases him.
His face is a yellow room.

Born twice, I see that the magazine in my lap is pointless.
I slip it into the seat pocket in front of me and settle down
For five hours of news flashes from my row partner's life.

"Jamaica will be good for Jen, my wife.
She's trying to lose some weight. The prospect
Of all that beach time will be an incentive."

And then,
                    "My gut's gonna go on strike if I
Don't get me some peanuts and a diet Coke."

And then,
                    "I sure hope those motel maids find my ring."

And then,
                    "What's going on up there?
Why are they getting up
And walking back this way?
Don't tell me the front bathroom is busted.
That's all we need. A backed-up line to the shitter.
Let me out. I'm gonna beat the rush!"

I am all too happy to let him out. Take your time,
I say, with this line-up you might not have another chance.
In his absence I experience a blessed moment,
Not of peace, exactly, no, just quiet. Maybe
Before he gets back I can fall asleep.

Last Thoughts

Like prairie dogs we
Sit up straight, pay attention.
No clouds in the sky.

*

Mom dials her cell phone
Hoping to reach Dad I guess
Before they stop her.

*

I wish I'd known this
Day would be my last. I'd have
Said so many things.

*

Autumn. A lovely
Season for a death song. Sing
As if you love Death.

*

Argument over.
Where we're going makes debates
Meaningless. Open.

*

Too bad we're not friends.
Our builds have much in common,
And your smile—so bright!

Baggage Compartment Cat

Cats are survivors,
Though I may be
The only one.
I'm no fan of flying
(who likes being jammed
in a cage and stuffed
on a dark shelf?)
But I've done it
Too many times
To let it worry me.

My human thinks
She can't live a week
Without me. Humans
Can be so sad.
This flight is ruined already
By the stupid dog that won't
Stop baying. He didn't get
Enough of the doggy tranquilizer.
It would be fun
To be a doctor to dogs.
What a shame!
So many mysterious overdoses.

This is something new.
The noise and heat
Are terrific. My fur
Is singed, and somehow
I am out of my cage,

On the ledge
Of a tall building.
I know this city!
I've been here twice
Before. It's raining humans!
Don't they know
We're too high,
That they never
Land on their feet?

This chaos is too much.
Down on the street
I'll scrounge some lunch.
I'm hungry! There's
Good eats in this town
For a smart cat.

Pest to Novel Reader

I've read that book.
How far are you?
                                        Huh?
How far? What do you think?

I'm sorry. What?
I have a hearing loss
In my right ear,
And with the noise
It's hard for me to make out
What people say.
I said What Do You Think!

About what?

About the book. Do you
Believe a tiger and a guy
Could really survive together
On a boat like that?

Why not? I mean, I guess.

It sticks with me
But somehow I
Don't buy it.

Oh, it's possible.
Anything can happen.

Yeah, especially in a book.
I wonder when
The movie will come out?

Maybe the author wants us
To think about
Unusual partnerships.

I guess. To tell
The truth, I never
Wonder about the author.
I read for entertainment,
Not to learn anything. Well,
Not consciously, anyway.
You know the part
I really didn't like?
When they finally
Get to land.
The tiger leaps ashore
And runs into the jungle
Without so much
As a thanks for the ride
Or look back
At the guy.
I guess
I wanted them
To stay together.
You know,
Going around

Having adventures
Like in a good dog story–
Only this time
It's a tiger.

They get to land?
                                        Huh?

I guess I haven't read that far.

Oh no! Now
I've gone and ruined
The end for you.
I'll just shut up.
Promise. Won't
Say another word.

Like Ethel and Fred

Something funny is going on.

Funny ha ha? Or funny weird?

Funny weird. Notice how the flight attendants
Are all bunched up? How come?

Maybe the microwave is on the fritz.
Maybe they're just gabbing, catching up
On the news before they get to work.

I've hit my call button three times and nobody's
answered.

They've got your number, troublemaker.

Very funny. I'm serious.

You're always serious. Or
Ridiculous, depending on your point of view.

Thanks for the support.

Come on! You know you're paranoid.

I can't help that I'm observant.

Yeah, right. Like when you thought
The mailman was stealing our mail?

Remember how you just knew
That the plumber stole your bowling ball?
And how about the time you were convinced
Your boss and I were having an affair?

So, maybe I was wrong a few times,
But I was right about the sprinkler.
Somebody else *was* moving it.

That's right. The kid down the block
Did that just to get your goat.

Ok, ok, Ms. Single Bullet Theory,
Mr. Reagan did nothing wrong selling guns to Iran.
The world's exactly as it seems.
Is that what you want from me?

Oh, honey, I want you to relax.
We're on vacation. Can't we enjoy the flight
And have a good time?
                                        Yeah, yeah.

I just want a cup of coffee,
Maybe a sweet roll.
                              I'm getting kind of hungry, too.
Oh, well, they'll be here soon.
What's going on up there?

Woman on the Run

Nothing could frighten me more
Than the life I'm running from.
I've seen the drug-sculpted scowl,
The fucked up genes
That made the man I thought
I loved a monster. He
Was such a charmer when
We dated in high school.
Bonnie my queen he called me,
And treated me like one.
Because he got me pregnant
I dropped out senior year.
We married quietly
And rented a little house
In a part of town that I'd
Avoided all my life.
He got a warehouse job
And I took care of Lou,
And one year later, Sam.
They kept me busy so
I didn't think a lot
About the things I'd missed.
I was late with groceries
The first time he confronted
Me about where I'd been. I guess
My answer wasn't good enough.
He hit me in the face.
He told me to watch myself,
That he knew what I was doing.

He said my galavanting
Days were over, that I
Needed his permission to leave.
The house. *Like hell*, I said,
But I soon saw things his way.
I had the kids to think
About; I wanted to live.
Looking back, I can't
Believe I called it living.
I mean, he made the house
Escape-proof. He took
The phone away. He blocked
The windows up and locked
The doors from the outside
When he left. He told me if
I tried to run away
He'd kill me and the kids,
And I believed he would.
He'd either changed, or was
The person I'd overlooked,
Enjoying my fantasy
Of love. We felt like moles
Penned up in there. A few
Times after rough-up sex
I pleaded for a change,
But that was always met
With rougher sex or beatings.
My spirit shriveled up.
My children never smiled.
So, what am I doing here?
I'm running for my life.
We got away because
My mom would not cave in
To my husband's threats. She called
An intervention group,

Which planned and carried out
Our escape. We crawled to freedom
Through a bashed in window.
I left a note for him
On the coffee table" *I*
Can't live like this no more.
Stay away, Bonnie.
They drove us to a house
In another town, and we
Decided mom would take
The kids while I'd go west
Until they figure out a way
To make him stop. You know,
Legally he hasn't
Done enough to get
Arrested–yet. I know
He'll kill me if he can.
So you see? I've been in Hell.
You can hang on there,
And you can makc it out.

Blamer

I blame Noah for the Flood.
He needed a reason to build a ship
Much larger than the Jones' sailboat.
I blame my boss for promoting
That idiot Dingle over me.
I blame my first grade teacher
For making fun of my stick figures;
For all we know, she blighted a brilliant career.
I blame public transit for spiking fares,
New York for phasing out those wonderful old cabs,
The vendor for slapping too much mustard on my bun.
I blame the coffeemaker down to its dregs,
And the toaster that won't stop burning my bagel.
I blame the highway department for year-old
Potholes on my street, and I blame
The Commissioner of Baseball for every day
He shows up at the office. I blame the sun
When it's too hot, the wind when I shiver.
I blame my friends who broke ranks and ran
Like mice, fearing their own cheese was imperiled.
I wish they could all be aboard. I blame
The president and his loudmouth vice president
For not being here personally to take charge
Of these thugs, and I blame you for this trip, these seats.
But I reserve the big blame for God,
Who answers to no one and explains nothing,
Who's going to get an earful before this day ends.

Turning It Around

I know. You think it's tough
Having to sit next to me
Because I spill out of my seat,
But I'm working on it. I was at
This clinic for people like me—fatsos.
It's ok. I can say it. It's me.
Anyway, I'm proud to tell
You I've already lost 23 pounds.
Can you believe it? In just a month.
My check-in weight was 335,
So I've got a ways to go before
I meet my goal—155
If you're interested. I know

You don't wish me ill by it,
But I'm familiar with that look.
You're thinking *why*? Why let yourself go
Like that? I was hungry, but not
For food alone. I wanted love,
Some recognition in my life.
Can you believe I was a beauty
Queen? It's true. In high school.
Well, I'm a planet or two from there!
But I'll get back. I'm dedicated
Now. I'm going to say goodbye
To wearing tents, goodbye to shopping
In those stores for ample women.

You know,

A lot of fat people were famous.

At the clinic they made us read about
Marlon Brando, and Orson Welles,
And that opera singer, Pavorotti.

My goodness they were handsome boys!
I tell you any one of them
Could eat crackers in my bed!
They had it all—success, fame—
But something, for sure, was out of whack.
In each of them there had to be
A hole he couldn't fill. I know
Something about that. I've got my own
That just got wider and deeper the more
I shoveled in to it.
                                        I know
Odds are I'll relapse. I'll hit a patch
In my life where I'll be bored or sad
And desperate, and all I'll want
Is everything bad to eat. I'll feel
Invisible, and so I'll try
To get attention by inflating
Like one of those spooky balloons
In the Macy's Thanksgiving Day Parade.
I know the odds, but I will try
My darnedest to beat them.
                                        Who knows? A year
From now we might meet up again
Like this, and you won't know it's me.
Then wouldn't you be surprised! I'd say
Remember me? The fat chick on
The plane? The armrest hogger?
You'll say you can't believe it's me.
Maybe you'll even ask me out!
Know what? I'd go. You're nice, a good
Listener, and I can tell

You wish me well. I'll reach my goal.
Say, when the flight attendant comes by,
I want you to take my pretzels, ok?

FLIGHT TWO

G. W. Among Us

How can I be here? Is this
Some–what do you call it–
Ulterior reality? Maybe
A couple of my old college cheers
Would get these guys on my side.
If I still drank beer
We could meet our minds that way,
But I'm committed to water,
Clean, green air, and my
Very special God, who should be theirs, too.
I oughtta get up there
To the cockpit and tell them
What's what. Say, I bet
I could fly this thing. After all,
I'm the Decider,
But my mind is all a-jumble;
My arms and legs won't move.
There's the Statue of Liberty
And New York's skyline–
The city that hates me.
Any minute now
I'm gonna do something bold,
Like my dad would do.
I like that saying
About the apple–what–
Falling on the tree.
Everybody's staring at me
Like they want something,
Like they're terrified, and pissed.

Executive Director

I log a hundred thousand miles a year
Across the states, promoting our agenda
For the arts, and often I'm asked if there
Is anything I fear. I say the cicada.
It's racket haunts my sleep. The questioner
Is always pleased. It fits the image of
Myself, administrative metaphor
Made flesh, the nation's art guru in love
With acting, painting, music, books, and you.
It's you I do it for (at great expense
To me), to save your souls, which never grew
Beyond the arid waste. You look so tense!
I'll let you in on a secret for your sake.
What keeps me sane? The difference *I* make.

Dr. Delusion

Why is it in a crisis people think
A doctor has cure-alls in a bag?
So many hold that image of a gent
As kind as Santa, who arrives by cad-

Illac to work miracles. I don't
Make house calls, and I don't especially
Warm up to seeing patients out of town.
Truth is I don't like seeing patients at all,

Never have. Some have a bedside gift,
But I do not. I knew it early, so
I spent a lot of time in office mode,
Directing things. What do I like best

About the field of medicine? The dough.
I mean to say, I love my sail boat,
My house on Cape Cod, my sprawling home
On the ninth fairway at the country club.

I love my wife, who gets the touch-ups that
She needs to look so young. I love my cars,
My kids—the fact they go away to school,
And I really love the hours. I go in when

I want. I work a hundred days a year.
Do I make more than I deserve? Who says?
Deserve's got nothing to do with it. I heard
That in a movie and said "right. That's it."

It's all we ever know. My parents told me
I should be a doctor. Since they paid
The bills I went along with it. That's smart–
To take advantage of your pedigree.

No questions, no debates. A troubled mind
Is poison. Don't apologize for who you are,
Just take advantage. Follow the blueprint.
One's available for every life.

The only thing I've got is valium.
Here. Pass it around. When we get out of this
I'll need some time alone at a resort–
A massage, definitely a manicure.

Never

I wish my lover
And his mother
From the sewer
Could join us here
For this disaster.
Thanks to them I'm over.

Having left to recover,
Perhaps relocate to another
City and job where
I'd revive my center,
I don't see how it's fair
To burn up in this hour.

There's so much fear
The cabin reeks. It's sour
With the odor
Of the giant loser
We're all part of. There.
I see the grinning Reaper,

And feel a surge of power
As we nose down, going faster.
I wish I'd been a grower,
Not the wrecker
I've become. I'm not together.
Not now, not ever.

Grim Commuter

A black cat
Stretched out
On the road
To the airport
Altered my mood,
Reminding me
That life is
Random   We're
All guilty
As hell   It
Wasn't me
But could have
Been had I
Been passing
The moment
That the cat
Left the hedge
Took a stride
Saw light   froze
I could say
I'd have swerved
To miss it
Better than
The killer
Sipping coffee,
Punching buttons
On his
Phone the road
Distracting

Oh God he
Might have said
To the phone
I think I
Hit a cat
Oh God he might
Have said again
Softly   but
God's nowhere
When you call
God's no 9 1 1
The day won't
Stop for grief
Its Planner
Is quite full
I drove by
My coffee
At my lips
Feeling sad
For the cat
Sadder for
Myself   for
All of us
Blundering
Through our lives
Killing what
Crosses us

UGLY AMERICANS, SO MANY

I can't believe you're telling me to sit
And shut my mouth. What's going to happen if
I don't? They're going to kill me? Kill us all?
Don't be ridiculous. It's just a grandstand play.
I see their type in D.C. all the time.
I mean, they're hard to miss. They stand out like
Lepers in a nudist colony.

Stop nudging me in the ribs. Go bite yourself!
They're lying when they say they've got the plane.
You think just anyone can fly these things?
You've looked into the cockpit as you've boarded
And seen the panels, switches, all those lights.
I couldn't begin to tell you how to fly
A plane like this, and I'm no dummy when
It comes to running things.
                                        These stupid punks
Don't stand a chance! You want to know what I think?
What's that? You don't? Well, listen anyway.
I say we're going to land, these A-rab jerks
Will leave the plane and get a hot surprise.
Then we'll be on our way. Publicity.
That's all these guys are after.
                                        Stop with the tears!
You're gonna make me jumpy if you get
All blubbery on me.
                                        Here comes one now.
Hey! Ali Baba! Turban Head! Yeah, you.
You ought to let my wife lie down somewhere.

Is first class full? Ok, I'll come with you!
No need to muss my shirt.
                    I'll be back soon,
After I talk some sense into these guys.
Ok, Saddam, take me to your leader.
You boys have no idea, the mess you're in,
But maybe I can help you out of it.
Americans can get you out of anything.

Fatalist

That all this trouble finds me now seems right.
I don't know why, but I've been summing up
My life, the things I've done and haven't done,
The solid fences and the broken doors.

For months the close of life has haunted me
Though I never saw it as a media
Event, just an exit unobserved
Except for those who'd find me. Don't you wish

That you could go like that? Of course, we want
To stick around as long as possible
Without great pain, though sadness, I'm afraid,
Seems unavoidable. I hate goodbyes.

I've wanted to cross over in my bed,
Serene, muttering some words
That like a beak breaks up my brittle shell.
We wish, and only wish, but get what comes

In spite of our best efforts to control
The world, the sun and moon, the spooky dark
That's all around us as we make our way.
It's in us, too. In every cell

We are the void, the hurricane and drought,
The sickness, vengeance, and the healing prayer.
We go together, but we wake apart.
Is that the truth? Will I ever know?

Blinded By Limerick

Don't shove! We're moving back.

Take away that knife,

You seem like a normal guy.

Middle Eastern, right?

Have you heard this one?

There once was a Saudi Arabian

Whose favorite actor was Fabian.

His pals called him looney,

They liked Mickey Rooney.

They wanted a reason to haze him.

Are you kind of like that guy?

Sometimes I feel that way,

You know, when your friends

Aren't really friends? Try this:

I once knew a guy, Juan Valdez,

Who wanted to wear a red fez.

He tried to steal Kiner's,

He shadowed three shriners

But never came up with that fez.

Or:

There once was a man from New York

Who hated being a dork.

He met a hijacker

Who threatened disaster

Then put out his eye with a fork.

Lilliputian

I'm small,
Have always been. Maybe
I can disappear
In this window seat.

The man to my left
Is hefty. He's
Spilling over the armrests.
It's comforting, his size

So close to me. It won't be
Quite so easy for the hijackers
To get to me.
                    When I was a girl
I played alone most days
And nights. The world,
It seemed, had little use
For an outgoing me.

That was all right. The world
In all its mammoth might
Was scary. I made my way,
As if among sparrows, mice,

The delicate Daddy Long Longs.
I built my secret places
In books, under apple trees,
Inside the clubhouse hollow
Of a blackberry hedge,

And all of them were good. I've
Always been a club of one,
And though I'm frightened

As we fly low over mid-town,
I feel these hijackers
Are also trapped in a club
Of one.
They're private,
Aren't they, like the twists
And turns of consequence
That shape our destinies?
The sky is a blinding blue.

Staring out the window
I catch my breath.
I feel invisible
And am amazed.

Nervous Flyer

I didn't used to be afraid.
When I was a boy I loved high places,
The higher the better. I saw myself
Atop a rocket heading for
The moon, and then a galaxy
No one had ever mapped before.
One time when I was eight
A friend dared me to jump off of
A second-story balcony
To a sloping lawn. I climbed the stairs
And didn't hesitate. I thought
Of Zorro, who was always doing
Shit like that. I landed funny,
And when I tried to stand my knee
Gave out, a fucked up hinge for life.
Was that when I began to fear
My death? Did I slip on the chains
Of earth, feel dizzy looking at
The stars? Now when I have to fly
I gulp a scotch and valium
Before I board, and have another
Drink as soon as the take-off light
Beeps off. Then if I cannot sleep,
A white-knuckled astronaut,
I sweat. I agonize and pray,
For all the good it does. I die
And die and die until we land.
I wobble off the plane ashamed,
A drenched, pathetic wreck, and vow
That's it, I'll never fly again.

Baggage Compartment Dog

I could have told them how this trip will end,
But who would listen to a kenneled dog?
A piece of baggage wedged into this hold,
I howl my head off. All that does is set the Pug

To yapping. That won't do us any good,
I want to say, but what's the use? Let's pray.
How many humans really understand?
When we go off, we're saying more than *Hey!*

The Labrador is so drugged up she sighs.
She's twitching in her sleep. I envy her.
She'll cross right over, never noticing
A difference. She'll feel no rush of terror

As we dive. I know what's going on up there,
And this: They won't remember us.

FLIGHT THREE

One Girl's Strategies

My mom said I was pretty, but not so bright,
Which limits what you can do in Indiana.
So I went to school to meet a guy
I'd maybe want to marry. I slept with two
Professors, which was a stupid thing to do.
I thought—what did I think—that they would see
The real me, the brilliant girl inside?
A little coaching would make me passable
At faculty parties, but I was kidding myself.
My lovers' colleagues smirked at me or tried
To sleep with me.
I got away from that
When I graduated, taking a job in town
As secretary for a pest control
Division of A&D. Good steady work
Agreed with me, but I was hungry for
Adventure, too. I wanted to see the world,
At least more of it than New Harmony,
Which has its points, but every burial mound
Is so familiar I see them in my sleep.

Two friends of mine from high school said I'd be
A perfect flight attendant, a natural.
I remember we were bowling, sipping beer,
When they laid out for me this glamorous life
Of travel to places I had only read about or seen on TV.

Some passengers are boors, but others are
A hoot, and every now and then we hook
Up on a lay-over. So here I am,
A knife pressed hard against my spine. I'm trained
To go along with hijacker demands,
But I wonder what I'll do when I am told
To open the cockpit door and stand aside.
This awful dream will end, I tell myself.
Just do what you're told. It's what you do so well.

Brothers of Dust to Dust

Ahmed, my skin is crawling.
I hate confined spaces, especially
When they're packed with infidels.

Be still! Don't call attention to yourself
By sounding like a crazy person.

Sometimes I want to say
Screw you to orders. But God is great,
And we are serving God.

Don't be impatient for heavenly reward.

Ahmed, If these are my last hours,
I want to spend them punishing our enemies.
I want them suffering as we have suffered.

We'll cleanse the world of their infection.
God has promised it.

That day can't come fast enough
When every infidel in every country
In the world goes up in flames.

Isn't that why we're here today?

It's our greatest day,
Our true birth day, Ahmed.

I want to mouth my prayers; you should do likewise.

Indeed, may we share
Our heavenly bounty
This day and forever, brother.

Reuben's Prayer

Lord, grant me a painless death,
A slipping out into
The vast beyond.
Make it seem to me
As cozy as a womb,
As soothing as her breath
Who slept by me,
And with me kept the land.
Assign me to the crew
That will be best for me.
Oh, let me live forever,
And living be at rest,
The itching powder of
My human time at an end.
Open your house to me
Who may have served you poorly,
But struggled to believe.
Reveal your face to me,
I pray, and your loving heart,
My first and only art.

Grandmother's Illness Narratives

I know it's silly, but
I wonder if I should
Handcuff my briefcase
To my wrist. For years
Grandmother's letters, the news
From 1918 when
She cared for victims of
Influenza, before
Taking sick herself and dying,
Spent decades in a drawer
Inside a plastic bag.
Good thing my mother lives
In Arizona where
It's dry. For years she never
Said a word about them, but
As soon as I discovered
Them while visiting
Last summer, it's all
She talks about. "Don't lose
The letters," she says in every
Conversation, as if
I hadn't thought of that.
Or, "You know they're all that's left
Of my mother, your grandmother."
The letters give
Details we've forgotten.
I never knew they burned
The sheets, sometimes the beds.
We don't remember how

So many died of thirst,
Or that their eyes would bleed,
That some, recovering,
Would try too soon to work
Only to fail again,
Most often fatally.
It was the plague reborn.
My mother blocked it out,
Her mother's illness narrative.
But now she won't let go. "You bring
Those letters back as soon
As you're done, you hear?"
I tell her they should be
In a museum or library collection,
But she's not having it.
"I want them back," she says.
"When I am dead I guess
You can do whatever you want."
I'll make some copies,
And then I'll take them home.

A Chattering Mind

Bladder rhymes with pancake batter.
Isn't it funny, the things the mind comes up with
When you drop the reins? It's like a leaf
On racing water. It doesn't care
Where it's going. I bet most of the time
That's just what it's thinking.

"I'm tired of thinking," the mind says.
"I want to float and drift on air currents like a bird."

Maybe next time I'll be a bird instead
Of all this earthbound power, which by the way rhymes
With *shower, cower, mower, blower, departure.*
So much seems wasted in these bubbleheads
In which we have to live.
When liberation comes,
When I escape the confines of this skull,
Just look for me all over. I'll be everywhere at once,
And all the time: A prickly breeze, a water spout,
A web up in the eaves. I'll be past harm,
Past everything that plagues this planet.
I'll be out of its misery
(which also rhymes with *mystery*).

A Wife Awake, Resolved

I'm really looking forward to the movie.
I haven't been to a grown-up film in what—
Five years? We don't have any sitters, you know,
No family nearby that we can call
To help us when we need to get away.
We joke, my husband and I, about the way
Our adult lives just ended when we had
Our first. Since then we've had two more because
Why not? In birthing class they never tell
You that your independent lives will go
Into a freezer for, oh, eighteen years.
Sometimes I laugh. I mean, it's obvious,
But you're so giddy with the project you
Don't think about the other stuff like no
More dining out at fancy restaurants,
No romantic weekends at the coast,
No staying up all night with videos
And making love in any room you want.
You can't escape those little sets of eyes.
They're always watching you, and don't believe
You ever know exactly what they think.
You care for them. You fret and work to pay
For all the things you think they need, for all
The things you want for them. It's mostly stuff
You think you wanted yourself when you were a kid
But never got, and then they're never as
Excited as you think they ought to be.
You work and shop. You cook and wash. You both
Collapse so you can sleep and get up fresh
And have a day just like the one before.

Then slowly you come up against the fact
Your husband seems a stranger in your bed.
I mean, you love him but you wonder who
He is. You know he's wondering the same.
You start to needle back and forth
And try to make some private space where you
Can breathe and maybe fantasize about
The cute guy in his twenties who changed your oil,
The one with tattoos and a nipple ring,
Who made you consider the unthinkable.
I'm sure my husband does the same at work.
He talks too much about the women who
Are so smart and independent. Once I called
Him on it and he got so mad at me
I thought, ok, we'll keep it to ourselves,
Which just creates more loneliness in us.
I took it till I couldn't take much more.
That's why I planned this trip, to clear my head,
To see if my priorities are straight.
I feel much better, too. Already I
Am missing him. I'm thinking of some things
That I can try to get us back to how
We felt before the weight of all this life
Bore down on us. We need to be more open
And less self-conscious, less willing to submit
To drudgery. We need to have more fun!
We need to say we're through with being ghosts.

Taser Maker

Ironic that I'm here like this, unarmed.
The taser maker. What I wouldn't give
To get my hands on one—the M26.
You'd see these punks turn somersaults. They'd bend
Like Gumby, and with a little luck they'd die.
The other day—you'll love this, we all got kicks
Out of it at the office—well, this guy in Bend
Goes bonkers. Snap, he's crawling in his pasture
Like a loco prairie dog. He bites and licks
The dirt. The cops show up. They're cautious, stumped.
Regardless what you hear, police don't live
To beat the holy crap out of the pricks
Who make a mess of things. I've seen them bend
Over backwards, keeping suspects alive
We'd rather see dead. Consider: The cops have sticks;
The bad guys are on drugs. They're crazed and armed.
I say you don't give scum like that a break.
Well, anyway—you say your name is Bev?
Hi, Bev. I'm Dex. I know, it rhymes with sex.
Well, back to what happened to that guy in Bend.
The cops tell him to cool it. He doesn't give
A hoot for them. He rolls around and kicks.
Before you know it, one of the cops gets decked
And that's when you don't want to be alive
If you're the guy. He gets the M26
Not once, but seven times! He jerks and flops
Like kids on an electric trampoline.
I mean, he goes insane. And then he died,
Which was fine. How many are there, Bev?
I counted six.

Dread

Hey, would you mind? Last time I checked, there's only one seat to a customer. Half of this armrest is mine, understand? *Mine.* Oh, spare me that look. Who do you think you are, Mother Superior? And by the way, I saw you take that magazine you've been reading out of the pouch in front of *my* seat. That makes it *my* magazine. Why don't you read your own? Look, the trick for someone like you, someone who is insensitive enough to plop down and spread out over more than one seat, is to think small. Think as tiny as you can. What? You don't like that? I'm supposed to be sad that you think I'm rude? Lady, if you were me you'd know that having to sit next to someone like you on an airplane is about as irritating as a feather up my nose. At least there's an end to this, which is more than I can say for the really awful things I have to deal with. Like what? Don't ask. Don't ask because you don't really care. This is heaven–isn't that a laugh!–compared to what I'm flying to.

Letter Home

My Darling Love,

I never told you well enough how dear you are to me. I don't know when they'll take this pen and book away, or if this paper will survive what's coming. We know from cell phones what's going on.

My Love, thank you for putting up with me. For all the times you forgave my glazed look, my inattentive listening, my drifting off in the middle of your favorite shows, snoring till you had to elbow me or hold my nose, thank you.

Thank you for holding my hand for hours after surgery, and for that small stream sound that came into your voice all those months of convalescence as you brought me back.

Tell Kate, when she misses me, to think of how we played this morning in her makeshift coffee shop before the shuttle came. Tell Joe to pick his grades up if he can, and always do what he wants to do. Tell Patrick to play the piano for me, because I'll be listening, and it will make me smile. I fear death, but I fear even more not coming home.

Not Quite Grounded

I know if I just sleep they'll go away.
The person sitting next to me is sweating
On my arm. I want to say excuse me, do
You mind? But would that get us anywhere?
He's terrified. Maybe we should pray.
I look around and see that some are doing
Just that. I should be joining them but go
Instead to the bathroom, or try, but there's
A hand all knotted in my hair. Today
I go along with it, surprised by this thing
That's growing in my gut, an icy floe.
I'm forced to the floor; the morning is so fair!
I see it through the window as we dive,
So urgent, earthward, marvelous, alive.

What Does It Mean?

After the terror, nothing.
After the strike, grief.
After grief, retaliation,
And after that, more
Suffering, more politics,
More posturing. We
Bought our tickets,
We paid our fares.
With our prejudice,
Votes, and indifference
We made this moment
Just as it is.
After the light,
After the bonding screams—
Nothing. Nothing I can
Make you understand.

Baggage Compartment, Dog Talk

When are we going to say we've had enough
Of being treated like afterthoughts? Let's tell
Them, Hey! We'd like some changes in our meals
Instead of the same thing over and over.
Do you ever watch their eyes when they feed us?
They're only present when they want our help.
They're grateful we lower their blood pressure,
But mostly they're unfocused.
                                        You're a bad
Dog, Carl, for saying such things. They take us in.
They keep us safe. They walk us, play with us
And take us to the vet. They even bring
Us on their trips—like this.
                                        Oh, Shep,
It's sad—the tripe you swallow, the news you miss.
How many tranquilizers did you eat
Before they kenneled you?
                                        How many what?
I ate some cookies I've never had before.

Of course you don't feel any different.

Well, I was sleepy till you started up.
What's with that smile? Stop shaking your head at me!

You are an empty page! Our humans put
Us in a pickle getting on this plane.
You haven't smelled the danger? Where's your nose?
If we survive this day I'm crashing out.

I'll roam the streets. I'll live up in the hills
Before I go on with this puppet life.
Hey, Shep. You still awake? It's just as well.
He'd never agree—the wrong species is caged.

She Dreams Her Way Across

Blindfold snug, I put my ear plugs in.
I love a drowsy take-off followed by sleep
That turns the turbulence to a rocker's peace,
To dreams that never were.
                                        My mother recovers
From her illness and lives to be a grandmother.
I see my father face himself, put back
The cork and drop the bottle in the trash.
My sister has second thoughts. She turns the key
To *off*, opens the garage door, and breathes.
The hills and meadows sparkle, green and gold.
Tomorrow I will lie under a zoo of clouds.
A year from now, I'll run in Spain.
And who approaches me?
                                        My college coach,
Who looks so serious while telling me
His secrets. His eyes are blue and desolate.
I want to tell him I will dedicate
Myself to train much harder than before,
But suddenly I'm six, a piglet girl
Stuffing herself on an uncle's wedding cake.
Then I'm older than the sun, or feel that way;
I'm inching closer to a dreamless sleep.
I'm going. Everything I know will go.
So natural in dreams to walk through doors.

FLIGHT FOUR

Flight Attendants Processing

I can't believe he broke up with you!

He says I'm gone too much,
He's sick of all my overnights.
He wants someone
To pay him more attention.

Tell him to get a therapist!

He's got one. She
Encouraged him. Wow!
Talk about misreading signals.
When he picked me up last night
He brought me flowers, and not
Just one of those florist specials,
But a bouquet he put together himself.
Why go to all that trouble if you're breaking up?

Feels guilty, I suppose. And he should.

I guess. Whatever.
My boyfriend loves
That I spend some time away.
He says it makes our relationship more intense.
I think he's right. It's nice
To have a lot of mini-breaks.

Looks like I'm going to get a longer break than that.
Why don't you get in touch

With that captain over at Southwest,
The one who kept calling you last year?
He's not married, and he's hot.

I don't know. Maybe. Do you
Ever have the feeling it's not worth it?

Not as long as I'm getting what I want.
Just put that dimwit bastard behind you,
Take some Yoga classes, and get back in the hunt.

Yeah, you're right. Do you want to take orders
While I stock the cart and mix?

Ok. Let's hit the aisle and get this over with.

A Pilot's Villanelle

I live to fly, to rise up nearer God
Who is my power and my confidante.
I do not fear the heavens or the sod

That stretch into infinities so loud
They each contain the chaos and the rant
Of those who fly to rise up nearer God.

These men who want the cockpit look so proud.
They're anxious, but not one appears reluctant.
They do not fear the heavens, or the sod

That seems a Never Land where sleepers brood
In frail dreams that seem so innocent.
Together we fly up, approaching God

Who waits for us where conflict is a load
We shake off like a wind-assisted plant
Shakes off a seed to heaven and the sod.

We'll be magnificent and never flawed.
May memories of us be clear, not bent.
We lived to fly, to rise up nearer God;
We did not fear the heavens or the sod.

Down, Down

What will I do at the end?
Will I think of friends I failed
Or friends who failed me? Will I
Think of my mother, long dead,
And wonder if I'll see her soon?
What would that be like? Would she
Be glad to see me, and I her?
What if the time between our visits
Is so vast we have nothing to say?

"You're here," she might begin. "I'm not
Surprised. Well, have a happy Afterlife!"

"Will you take me around?
Show me the ropes?"

"Sorry, but I hardly know you now.
You'll figure it out. The rules
Are different. Nothing
You did before matters here."

"You mean we start all over? Fresh?"

Or will I flash on all the things
I think I'll miss...like Breyer's
Butter pecan ice cream, Bob Edwards
On NPR at 6:30 every morning,
A summer day at the temple,
Lulled by bells. Will I miss

The sun coming and the sun going?
The moon and its promise of love,
Then love lost? What will I be thinking
When I'm blinded by impact and light?

Sparring Partners

We've been married forty years,
Which makes us old to everyone
But us. We met in Idaho
After the Korean War.
At first she didn't warm to me
Because I talked too much about
The places I'd been and all my plans.
"Hot air," she said. "A lot of gas."
Of course, I realized later on
That was her way when she was flirting.
Ouch! Don't pinch me, dear. As I
Was saying, she didn't like me much,
But pickings were slim in Idaho,
So she was willing to give me a chance.

Don't listen to this geezer if
You want to know the truth. He lies.
He's always been a fibber
Though it never broke us up.
I guess we've been compatible.

Forty years! You *guess*? That's all?
You see what I've put up with since
The day she collared me. I swear—
Living with a headstrong wife

Is challenging—like taking hills
That don't belong to you. That makes

Me think about the war. MacArthur
And I were studying a map
When Doug, he says to me–
Oh, here
We go again. He knew them all,
The high command. They couldn't make
A move without the wizard's thoughts!

Do you mind? I'm telling a story here!
Your opinion doesn't count because
You were never there.
Were you? Are you sure?

That's cruel. You've seen my Purple Heart,
My regulation boots. You know I served
My country, did my duty, while you
Were safe, sleeping in flannel sheets.

All right. Don't have a heart attack.
It's true that you were in the war.

Ok, now that's settled be still
And learn a thing or two. Let's see.
What were we talking about? Oh, yeah,
The time I cowboyed in Idaho.
Now that was fun, but hard work, too.
We'd rodeo on Saturdays
And I became World Champ on bulls.

I had to give that up when I
Was hired by the FBI to work
As a rural operative. I knew
The terrain, you see. Those city feds
Were blind without me.
You need to get out?
Oh, sure. I'll finish when you get back.
Nice fella, that.
You drove him off,
You fool, with your bragging and your chatter.

Oh, what does a wrinkled old woman know?
I swear, as soon as we get down
I'm calling a service to trade you in
For someone younger, the sweeter model
You never were.
That's fine with me.
I'll help you dial. I'll interview
My liberator, tell her what
A great old bag of gas you are,
And wish you well. I really will.
What are you laughing at? Not me,
I hope, because I'll bop you good.

I'm laughing at the both of us.
Forty years and counting...I guess
We'll never stop.
Well, not until
I'm standing on your grave.
You mean
Beside my grave.
I mean what I said.

The Writer and the Candle Maker

So, my stories aren't the stuff the *Times* smiles on.
My sister on her farm outside Raleigh
Likes them. My mother used to phone
To tell me that once again I had bested
Hemingway, and my girlfriend
(who took my class for three semesters)
Says that they'll be reading me
Long after I'm dead. I wonder
If that really comforts me.

Are you a writer?

Huh?

A writer. I see you're writing in that book.
I asked if you're a writer.
Yes, I am.

Well, what's your name? Have I read your stuff?

I doubt it.
Come on! Don't be shy.
I'm reading all the time. I love good books.

It's...Clemens. Sam. There. You see?

Clemens? I've heard of you! But you're a pitcher,
Not a writer, ain't that so?

That's Roger, not Sam. I'm not the pitcher.

Oh, yeah, it is Roger, isn't it.
You said your name is Sam. I guess
You're right. I haven't heard of you.
But hey, that's all my fault, not yours.
So tell me what you write.

Pep talks.
I write pep talks to myself. Sometimes
I imagine I'm an animal
Gone mad. I murder people I don't like
(I close my book and fasten up my tray).

Don't be that way. We're stuck here side by side.
What did we say when we were kids in the play house?
You show me yours, I'll show you mine.

Look–
Linda's my name. I come from a town
Called Mur, well, Murray, Kentucky's the map name,
But all of us from there just call it Mur.
And you?
I'm sorry. What?
Where you from?
Hastings-on-Hudson, a place you've never heard of.

It's on the Hudson River. Am I right?

A lucky guess. Ok, Lisa–
Linda—

Linda, what do you do (I want to say,
besides harassing your fellow passengers)?

My husband and I make candles on our farm.

We've patented a secret formula
For candle wax. We sell them everywhere,
Our candles, I mean. I bet you've burned a few
With special dinners and such. So tell me is
It true that writers really know how to cook?

They know how to eat, how to sponge, and how to order
Off a menu.
Oh, you're pulling my chain,
Or should I say my noose! I'm kidding. Say,
Why don't you show me what you're working on!
Here. An even trade. That's our catalog.
You look through that, and I'll just look through you.
Maybe you'll find some candles you can't live without.
Maybe we'll trade! My candles for your books!
Maybe you'll find something to write about.

(I want to say, *you are preposterous,*
but then I think, *she's asking to read your work!*)
Ok.
I pull my latest story-in-progress
From my satchel under the seat. I take
Her catalog and plunge into its pages
Wondering if she'll like what I've handed her,
Or if she'll start to fidget, desperate to
Get out of this. Without looking I pat her hand.
The catalog is pleasing. Not half bad.

Formidable

Take your hands off me! I'm a Hellcat.
I'll yank the eyes right out of your head.
I'll make your Momma rue the day
She pushed you out into this world.
I ain't in no hurry to get to the next one;
You shouldn't be, either, because
I bet it won't be anything like what we think,
And it might be one hell of a lot worse.
Then won't you be sorry!
                                        Don't push!
I'll spin your pecker head around backwards.
I got by all those crackers in Alabama
And I can sure get by the sorry ass likes of you!
I've buried my Momma, my brother and sister,
My husband and three children of my own.
I've cried more tears than there's water in the ocean,
But none of that, and none of you,
Will shut me up or keep me down.
I raised eight kids, and five of them went to college.
I've lived on the streets, I've been on and off assistance;
I beat the dealers off my block.
                                          I've been down on my knees
Praying for a miracle, and down there scrubbing floors
For minimum wage. I've lived out of dumpsters
And stood in line five hours for a free Christmas turkey
And a toy for each of my kids. I've shopped so much
In the Dollar Store I should have me some stock in it.
I never owned a car. I don't drive,

But I can walk anywhere, and do.
I'm free to climb as high or sink as low as I want. I can be
Mean as hell, and I can be your sweetie pie.
How you treat me determines what you get. So
Don't be putting hands on me in no bully way,
And stuff your cheap shit jive about America.
I *am* America!

Actor

For seven years
I showed up
For cattle calls,
Played bit parts
In off off
Off off shows.
I bussed tables,
Ate Saltines snitched
From coffee shops,
Slept with women
Twice my age
For money, gifts
That made me
Feel as if
I were someone.
I bounced checks,
Borrowed money I
Could never repay.
If I slept
Alone, I slept
On couches, benches,
Sitting up, standing.
I sold drugs
Until a roommate
Overdosed. I put
The needle in.
His sister said
Don't take it
Too hard. He

Was drug death
Waiting to happen.
Thanks, I said
And hurried to
the audition that
Changed my life.
I'm heading west
To play in
A nighttime series.
That's why this
Can't be right.
We need someone,
A director, to
Yell *Cut!* and
Change this scene.

God Baby

In one month
I would celebrate
My first birthday.
My parents cry
Because I won't
Ever be old.
They think that
I don't know
What's going on.
It comforts them
A little, but
They don't realize
An infant sees
Everything, that for
A time we
Possess God-sight until
The portal closes.
I will exit
This body with
That sight intact.

Touch

Nerves going off like fireworks;
Looks on human faces
That other humans shouldn't see;
Cell phones rioting–
I hate the one that sounds
Like a stricken cat.
The baby three rows up
Wailing like a banshee;
The scuffle in the galley;
A stewardess slumping to the floor;
The plane descending;
My neighbor digging her nails
Into the armrest until I offer her my hand.

The Power of Intention

I wonder if machines have souls, and if
That's so, what happens when we make them do
What they're not made to do? Does that bother you?
I saw a movie once that stuck with me.
Some scientists wrote words on water tanks;
They wrote out words like *love* and *peace* and *hope*.
The water's molecular structure in those tanks
Assumed fantastic shapes, harmonious
And beautiful as snowflakes and wild flowers.
On other tanks they wrote *I hate you, die*,
And other words that make us look away.
Those branded molecules of water took
On grotesque shapes that pulsed with anger. They
Were horrible to look at.
Don't you see?
If water has a soul, why not a plane,
My purse, your lap-top, even your chewing gum?
You want to act? Why don't we pass the word
To write on folding trays and seats in front
Of us, on windows and window shades, on wall
And ceiling panels, even on the floor.
Let's cover the plane with words like *love* and *peace*.
Let's write them on ourselves. Give me your arm.

ON THE GROUND

Elementary School

These classroom chairs are small,
The kids are loud and whiney.
I wish I'd stayed in bed,
I was dreaming about money.

Power's funny, too,
The way it comes and goes.
My God! This teacher's got
A pretty, upturned nose.

I'd better say some things
To look more presidential,
But not so much that I
Appear too deferential.

Does that mean caring? Meek?
I'm also strong and loving!
I wish I was at the ranch,
Alone, just out there running.

I'm really in great shape,
No fat, no complications.
I wonder if my guy
Made dinner reservations.

How long does this go on?
Am I stuck here for an hour?
Don't fidget. Don't sound dumb,
Don't look too stern or sour.

Now what? It's story time?
Oh, man. Don't make me read!
Oh, good! It's teacher's turn.
Before I do I need

Some time to get it right,
To get in the mood, prepare.
Reading isn't easy.
Who's whispering in my ear?

That's great. No golf today.
I need a long vacation.
The country's under attack,
Somebody make a decision!

Do I go here or there?
What are my people doing?
Don't interrupt the teacher.
What's that? The goat is going?

I guess I should be, too,
But not until the story
Ends. How long can it be?
I hope it isn't gory.

Maybe if I sit here
Peaceful in my book
They'll come and tell me, Oops!
We've had another look

At all those scary reports
And found they're just mistakes.
He's back again. Oh, darn.
Ok. Well, that's the breaks.

I'm sorry, kids, but I
Will have to leave you now.
Mind if I take the book?
I'll finish it, and how!

Well, get me out of here!
Where's the nearest bunker?
Call my mom and dad.
Tell them to take cover.

The country's blowing up?
Who'd do a thing like that?
Don't tell me! I can guess.
It's that Saddam. Iraq!

Ok, let's fly around
Until we get a plan.
Be sure it's covered up,
How we panicked, how we ran.

We'll tell them that we hid
To fight another day.
That's it! This is our chance,
Invade. We'll make them pay.

West Chester, New York

It was as if he said *Come at me, Man!*
I've never seen a squirrel so irate.
I froze in my driveway, wondering if he
Would really attack. He thumped his right paw on
The fence, insistent, vexed, making his point:
What right have you to park beneath my tree?
I thought of offering nuts, but what if he
Decided they made perfect missiles to
Fire back at me? He huffed and coughed and barked
As I stood still, not knowing what to do,
Too deep inside his world, yet not so far
I understood, or felt much confidence
That he would turn away and let me pass.
I praise the squirrel who made me miss my flight.

Prayers & Mantras

Om mani padme hum Om mani padme hum Om mani padme hum

"Om Mani Padme Hum" (pronounced Om Ma-ni Pay-may Hum) is the mantra of Avalokiteshvara (Chenrezig)–the Bodhisattva of Compassion.

*

"The innocent and the beautiful
Have no enemy but time;
Arise and bid me strike a match
And strike another till time catch;" -W.B. Yeats

*

This is the text of the 100-syllable mantra of Vajrasattva, a symbol of the mind's inherent purity.

oṃ vajrasattva samayam
anupālaya
vajrasattva tvenopatiṣṭha
dṛḍho me bhava
sutośyo me bhava
supośyo me bhava
anurakto me bhava
sarva siddhiṃ me prayaccha
sarva karma su ca me
cittaṃ śreyaḥ kuru hūṃ
ha ha ha ha hoḥ
bhagavan sarva tathāgatavajra

mā me muñca
vajrī bhava mahā samaya sattva
āḥ (hūṃ phaṭ)

*

Rabbana ighfir lana dhunubana wa israfana fi amrina
Our Lord, forgive us our sins and our excesses in our affairs.

*

Hail Mary, full of grace, the Lord is with thee.
Blessed art thou among women, and blessed is the fruit of thy womb, Jesus.
Holy Mary, Mother of God, pray for us sinners, now and at the hour of our death. Amen.

*

Dear Goddess, help me, lovely Lady,
To put love where there is hatred
To put hope and faith where there is doubt
To put joy where there is discord
Please help me to heal my pain
Help me learn the spirit of forgiveness
Grant me your divine wisdom
So that I can love and be loved again.
I ask this in the Lady's name, so be it!

*

Have mercy on me, oh God, according to your steadfast love;
according to your abundant mercy blot out my transgressions.
–*Psalm 51:1*

*

Samam sarveshu bhutesu tishthantam parameshvaram, vinashyatsv avinashyantam yah pashyati sa pashyati (Sanskrit from The Bhagavad Gita, English below)

One who sees the Supreme Lord equally present in all beings, the imperishable within the perishable – that person truly sees. The hallmark of genuine realization is the perception of the Divine equally in all forms of existence.

About the Author

Written over two decades, *The Excellent Assembly* commemorates the 25th anniversary of 9/11. These fictive lyrical narrative poems and monologues remember the dead, the survivors, and those whose heroism inspires us to this day.

McDowell is recognized as a central figure in New Narrative and New Formalist Poetry. His formal and free verse poems always bring together lyric and narrative elements that make for a reading experience like no other. His poems appear in anthologies, journals, magazines and newspapers around the world; his books have appeared from Henry Holt & Company (Owl Books), the University of Pittsburgh Press, Penguin, Free Press/Simon & Schuster, Peterloo Poets (England) and The Salmon Publishing in Ireland.

McDowell teaches at Kent State University, and taught at the University of Southern Indiana, UC Santa Cruz and the Bennington low-residency MFA program, which he co-designed with the late Liam Rector. With Mark Jarman, he created and co-edited *The Reaper*, an influential literary magazine. McDowell was also co-founder, editor and director of Story Line Press, where he selected and guided into print more than 300 books.

www.ingramcontent.com/pod-product-compliance
Lightning Source LLC
Chambersburg PA
CBHW032055140826
49883CB00028B/265
9781950475490